MW01505907

The Unfortunates

LIBRARY
NEW HAMPSHIRE
INSTITUTE OF ART

THE UNFORTUNATES

POEMS BY WILLIAM BAER

NEW ODYSSEY PRESS

KIRKSVILLE, MISSOURI

PS
3552
.A3324
U5
1997

First New Odyssey edition published 1997
Copyright © 1997 Thomas Jefferson University Press
All rights reserved
Printed in the United States of America

Author photo by Jesika Brunk
Cover illustration is *The Little White Girl: Symphony in White No.2* by James Whistler, reproduced by permission of Tate Gallery, London/Art Resource, NY.

Some of the poems collected in this book were first published as follows: "Fire Watcher" in *Amaryllis;* "Malta" in *The Chariton Review;* "Obituary in *The New York Times,*" "Aliens," and "Telephone Psychic" in *Chronicles;* "Hospital" in *Hopewell Review;* "The Cuban Girl" in *The Hudson Review;* "Breaking and Entering" in *Janus;* "South Shore Cottage" in *The Lowell Review;* "Runway" in *The New Press Literary Quarterly;* "Main Reading Room" and "Crematorium" in *The New York Quarterly;* "Documents" and "Nightflight" in *North Dakota Quarterly;* "East River" in *Orbis* (England); "Adriatic" in *Ploughshares;* "Books" in *Poetry;* "The Shipmaster's Note" in *Poetry Nottingham* (England); "Hospitals" in *Poetry Wales;* "Country Club" in *Quadrant* (Australia); "Suicide Note" in *The Swansea Review* (Wales); "Munich" in *The Tennessee Review;* "Sea of Marmara" and *"A Rebours"* in *Verse.*

Library of Congress Cataloging-in-Publication Data

Baer, WIlliam, 1948–
   The unfortunates : poems / by William Baer.
     p. cm.
   ISBN 0-943549-46-9 (hb : alk. paper). — ISBN 0-943549-47-7 (pb : alk. paper)
   I. Title
PS3552 . A3324U5 1997
811' . 54—dc21

                                             97-11544
                                              CIP

New Odyssey Press is a division of Thomas Jefferson University Press at Truman State University in Kirksville, Missouri 63501 (*http://tjup.truman.edu/newodyssey*).

No part of this work may be reproduced or transmitted in any format by any means, electronic or mechanical, including photocopying and recording, or by any information storage or retrieval system, without permission in writing from the publisher.

The paper in this publication meets or exceeds the minimum requirements of the American National Standard—Permanence of Paper for Printed Library Materials, ANSI Z39.48 (1984).

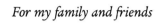

For my family and friends

CONTENTS

· I ·

· 2 ·

· 3 ·

· 4 ·

Now all of this, from the beginning, the good merchant could not but consider rather hard for the unfortunate man.

—Melville

I

CULTS

North of Redding, off the interstate,
he sat on the roof of his Porsche in his wrinkled suit
and watched the cars zip by into the sun.
Sister Sarah's letter, about the Prophets'
Retreat in Shasta Forest, lay in his lap.
Four days ago, he hadn't shown up for work—
to cruise Route 5 from Hilt to Santa Ana
and back again—trying to settle his mind.

Years ago at college, in Ann Arbor,
amid the drugs and sex, another Sarah
had ditched him for a lying friend; so three
weeks later, he went to the "weekend seminar"
for lectures, singing, prayers, discussion groups,
and mindless chants, sleep deprivation, guilt,
and indoctrination. He'd never been so happy.
He dropped from school, and cut his parents off.

[handwritten: → Unfulfilled by hedonistic lifestyle]

He worked from 8 till 8 for Father-Master,
selling flowers in the malls and luring
new recruits away from broken homes
and loveless lives—who found the commune full
of friends and purpose, occult mysticism,
and tranquil social visions for the future.
They also found, he knew, the comforting belief
that they were better people than everyone else.

[handwritten: Seduced by false gods and utopianism]

Two weeks before his Master chose his mate,
he was abducted to a sealed motel
by Mr. Starks, deprogrammer, employed
by his parents. He recanted three days later:
Yes, the Master owned a New York mansion,

limousines, hotels, and a fifty-foot yacht.
Yes, he'd been brainwashed. Yes, the Master had said,
"I'll subjugate the world. *I am your brain.*"

The "Family," once, had broken him in; now Mr.
Starks had broken him down. He went back home
to Battle Creek, completed his degree,
sorted mail, married, and fathered a child.
But suddenly, it fell apart; he wasn't
sure why, although they both had countless flaws,
and often, when Cindy was there, she really *wasn't*—
until she started talking about divorce.

The day they split, he drove to Arizona,
and found the Siblings of the Holy Place,
and Moses Burke, messiah, who spoke with God
and Krishna, Buddha, Luther, and even Caesar.
"Forsaking all," he fell in quickly with
the rituals, millennialism, disclaiming
in tongues, astrology, polygamy,
and patrolling their borders with AK-47s.

Mr. Starks once said that cults provided
the security of everlasting childhood.
Which was true, and exactly why
he felt content again, until Darlene,
one of the Savior's teenage concubines,
shot HIM through the eyes and wrecked it all.
Everyone scattered, even his Sibling "wives"—
all three—who suddenly grew ashamed and vanished.

He sat in the dust, for several days, and stared
at the Copper Mountains. Finally, since both his parents
were dead, he rose and drove to California—
resolved to try <u>a normal life</u> again:
an M.B.A. at Davis, a high-tech job
in San Mateo, a condo on the bay,

a closet full of suits, and a loyal pretty
woman, dressed in chic designer clothes.

He was a man who possessed everything:
the perfect, rehabilitated life.
So why, last month, did he write to Sister Sarah
after the *San Francisco Chronicle* had run
its condescending piece on the Shasta Prophets?
And why had he been driving up and down
the interstate? And why did this piece of paper
in his lap feel like the key to the kingdom?

Mysticism and Spiritualism
fill the existential Void in
his heart

2

SEA OF MARMARA

The wire came, with death, to Istanbul:
"The ship would not arrive." For six full days,
she softly walked, amid the seven hills,
and past the Ottoman's ancient palace walls,
watching the minarets of Santa Sophia,
thinking only of him, her handsome cousin,
and that he would, of course, be safe, and yet,
never once, did she look upon the sea.

But now the city wailed for those now drowned—
as she lay in her fever, in her room,
until one day, she came down to the sea.
And there was the Bosphorus and its Golden Horn,
and there was the clear blue Sea of Marmara,
and everyone watched its mesmerizing waters—
but she just watched the sky, so dreadfully blue,
lifeless, but wishing, like him, to be her friend.

Breaking and Entering

When he was done, he sat in their living room:
as always, he'd made certain they'd be away,
and checked for dogs, alarms, and nosy neighbors,
then glass-cut through a window in the back—
ready with the knife he'd never used
(but would)—and quickly packed her gold and stones,
their small antiques, and the "knock-out" Tiffany lamp—
which these dull bastards certainly <u>didn't deserve</u>.

But he liked their quiet house, just as he'd liked
his parents' best when they were sound asleep,
no nagging, fighting, or banging him about.
Some "sneaks" enjoy the breaking in—"like sex"
they say—while others crave the risks, or just the goods,
but he liked sitting in their living rooms,
until, at last, he'd slit their couches open, and leave.
Too bad. He liked it here; it felt like home.

HOSPITAL

A noise. And she awakes alone into the dark,
and feels the anesthetic in her veins
and all the catheters, and IV lines,
and other things still keeping her alive.
Unable to move, she watches the monitor lights,
strange blues and reds, of countless medical machines.
Her operation's done, and now she cries—
maybe, one might think, from pain or fear.

But she recalls that summer in her youth,
and how they raced across a lovers' Europe,
and how they loved, especially in Spain,
until the little quarrel in Barcelona—
and how she woke alone the very next day,
and he was gone, for good, forever,
and she refused to cry, until right now—
one might survive disease, but never that.

PROSECUTOR

Another homicide, another trial.
He hated every single bit of it.
So why did he still bother? He seldom saw
his wife these days; his paycheck was a joke;
and the boss was nothing but a petty party hack
scheming to be governor. It also
wasn't the murder scenes, the sleazy lawyers,
soft judges, lying witnesses, and timid juries.

It also wasn't some personal vendetta
against the thugs, the whores, and all the psychopaths.
Even noble notions about "justice"
weren't enough anymore. But still, he knew why,
watching the trembling, devastated father
of the dead Hispanic girl
—battered, raped, stabbed over 25 times—
unable to hold his shaking cup of coffee.

LIBRARIAN

Once she liked to log and stack the books
in order—perfect and neat—all the marvelous books
so full of wisdom, both comprehensible
and far beyond her grasp. She'd disciplined herself
to tolerate the patrons, but things had gotten worse.
The "dolt" percent had risen fast: "Where's
the latest diet book?" or "Nostradamus?"
or "water sports?"—not exactly Milton or Plato.

But she, herself, had also changed, especially since
she'd dumped her Jack for Steve and lost them both.
Lately, even the books were getting on her nerves.
So she began to sneak the classics home
at night—no one seemed to notice—
and buy the garden hoses, because tonight
she planned to soak this place real good—
into a swamp of swollen, damp, disgusting books.

BELMONT

12,000 bucks on Red Dust in the 5th.
Everything they'd ever saved. But he didn't
tell his wife, and bore the burden alone,
a decent man who *never* bet, who *never* believed
in so-called "sure things," but knew the mob believed
in nothing else. So when he'd told Mr. R.,
near the loading dock, about his oldest boy's
financial troubles, the man had mentioned the race.

And Mr. R. was always right. But at the gun,
at 6-1, Red Dust, as the race began,
just froze in the gate. In shock, unable to breathe,
he stared at the horse, while somewhere else,
near the finish line, Neon hit the tape.
So he sat in the stands for hours, a fool and sucker,
until he learned the rules about "non-starters":
he'd get his money back, but not much else.

NIGHTFLIGHT

Forty thousand feet above the ocean,
flying to the islands, everyone sleeps,
in the high-altitude hum, except for her.
Her mind won't rest. She's thinking about
everything they'll do when she arrives:
walking the beach at Waikiki; dinner
in Honolulu; visiting Pearl Harbor
and Diamond Head; then sailing on Kahuna Bay.

Over and over, she runs it through her mind,
everything they'll do, everything they'll say,
aware that even when they do these things,
they'll still be thinking of what comes next,
forever lost in dreams of future time.
Exhausted, she looks out through her window.
She needs to escape. The only rest is sleep,
which is, as she knows, just more of the same.

FIRE WATCHER

Watching the fire flash across the roof,
he catches the smell of lacquer in the air:
another "Class B" fire, most likely arson,
dangerous and tough to extinguish,
insanely hot, with blasts of jet-black smoke.
Then, suddenly, the right side wall gives out,
incendiary flame engulfs the roof,
rising with its beauty in the night.

Yes, it gives him pleasure, when no one's hurt,
to come and watch. So all night long, he waits
in bed, listening to his radio.
He knows the captain thinks he fits the profile:
lonely, male, stupid, and insecure—
the captain says, "If he hasn't yet, he will."
But it's not true. He doesn't even light
his stove; he keeps no matches in his house.

GARBAGE

She sorted though it very carefully:
the coffee grounds, the high-fat foods, the filters
of his cigarettes—*He's smoking again*—
a new rosé, her favorite shaving cream—
she smelled the empty can—the same junk mail
he'd gotten for years. Until the restraining order,
she used to follow him everywhere he went,
then, for a while, she stole his mail.

Her useless friends discarded her as well:
"Modern women don't behave like that."
Well, maybe not. She pushed aside some canceled
checks. What's this? A woman's business card.
Maybe that slinky blonde from Queens? She flipped it over:
"Stay the hell away from my garbage, you sicko!"
She jolted back, in shock and fear: *He knows!*
Now she couldn't even trust his garbage.

· **3** ·

DRAINAGE PIPE

Yesterday, before things really happened,
he stared down into the blackness of the hole,
8 inches wide and, now he knew, some 30
feet deep, an old, forgotten drainage shaft
of nothing: no cries, no whispers, no nursery rhymes,
but she was down there somewhere, just like that "Alice"
the teacher had read about at school, but this
one stuck, and didn't come out the other side.

But now, with all the excitement, he'd put the baby
out of his mind for fire trucks, and tractors,
TV cameras, rat-hole rigs, and cranes,
jackhammers, carbide drills, and far more people
than ever seen before in Winston, Oklahoma.
He figured, being eight years old, he could enjoy
it more than all the rest—and most of all,
that pretty lady from the nightly news.

For now, he liked to wander through the crowd
and listen, especially near the pit and the working men—
"We busted another tungsten bit."—
"Where the hell's that hydro-drill?"—
"Get those Hollywood creeps away from here."—
And one passed out in the August heat, another
puked in the grass, and one big driller cried
when Becky sang from the shaft: "Rock-a-Bye, Baby."

"He's over here!" He heard her pretty voice
and smelled her strong perfume, then turned around
into the TV camera. "You ready, Stevie?"
she asked, as someone quickly combed his hair,
as others moved him closer to the pit,

just because he'd told her he was "Baby
Becky's" cousin, just because he wanted
to be on television. No harm in that.

It happened very fast. He told her that
Rebecca'd be "OK," and that her parents
were "very brave," but she was disappointed.
"What's Becky's favorite toy?" the woman tried.
"Raggedy Ann," he conjured out of nowhere.
She smiled; he understood. "I think she had the doll
when she fell in." They all stood stunned. "Guess what?"
"What, Steve?" "I taught her 'Rock-a-Bye.'"

The woman slipped five dollars in his pocket,
and then they were gone. He sure enjoyed appearing
on TV, even though he'd never really met
the baby's parents. But he'd seen them both around,
and just last night, he'd watched them on TV
and they were very brave, and perfect, and asked for prayers.
He'd also seen them, last summer, dancing close,
and laughing, at the Randall Country Fair.

"Shouldn't you be getting home now, son?"
Mr. Reicher asked him, later in the night
during his drilling break, so Stevie nodded
and walked beyond the range of the huge spotlights.
His mother'd be lying around with her latest boyfriend,
who couldn't care less where he was, as long as it
was out of sight, but at least he didn't bother
to belt him around like her last one had.

So he sat alone, high on a nearby mesa
and watched them work, in front of the TV cameras,
for over an hour, as they got closer and closer,
willing to do most anything to save that girl.
Anything. He wished that, later, walking home
he might, like Becky, fall in such a hole,

so everyone could come and rescue him, or maybe,
like Alice, he'd come out on the other side—in Wonderland.

He jolted awake from drifting into sleep,
as a filthy man was hoisted from the pit.
Alone. They'd have to widen the "horizontal shaft."
Everyone was very disappointed, and Stevie,
who'd never learned to pray, just wished the girl
would come up soon—then rose and walked away
toward home. He'd better get some rest: that pretty
TV lady might need him in the morning.

4

The Cuban Girl

Perhaps tonight. Except this city night
is nothing but an eerie, shadowed maze ....
He wanders through the lower eastside streets
confused, without the pain, and strangely calm,
searching under the bluish city lights,
wanting very little, just another glimpse
across those decades lost and unredeemed.
But nothing at all is the same. He's waited too long.

But then, across the street, he sees the girl
who looks like *her*. Lovely, she passes by,
though far less beautiful. It seems, for him,
there's nothing left, until he stops and hears,
hears something he recalls—a distant rumble
lightly shakes the ground, the subway fades
away—the night is empty once again,
he feels his cancer move. Perhaps tonight.

Magnum XL-200

Cedar Point, Ohio

For maximum speed, he rode the Magnum
fully loaded at 3:13, the hottest time
of the day. It ripped, from its crest, down the 195
feet at 60° and 73 miles per hour—
at 3.55 g, like the turns at Indy.
Two minutes later, he couldn't get out of the car,
sitting helpless, pale and suffocated,
listening to his strange arrhythmic heart.

Sure it was embarrassing: an overweight, middle-
aged man who spent his vacations riding roller coasters.
But he didn't care. The panic distracted his mind
from his boring job, the inconsiderate wife,
and their whacked-out, dropped-out, wise-assed, teenage sons.
So he'd never even mentioned the mitral valve prolapse.
If it happened, it happened, which, five months later, it did,
on the Coney Island Cyclone, a mile from home.

MALTA

Who knows why she came and never left?
For fifteen years, she's walked these Maltese coasts
surrounded by the endless dark blue sea.
And some would say it's just her refuge from the world,
as once it was for banished Cicero.
But others would say she's running from her past,
a "wild American beauty," just seventeen,
who'd left behind some badly broken lives.

But others say she's waiting for the sea
to finally give her back her only lover,
his body never found, who drowned beneath
the rocky cliffs on the coast above Valletto.
Still others say, with knowing looks, she never
leaves because she's frightened of the water.
But early tonight, just before she vanished,
we saw her walking alone at the water's edge.

DOCUMENTS

He shifts his weight, and avoids the blonde.
He's standing on a line that hasn't moved
in many hours. Maybe even days.
The blonde is on Line B. She gestures again.
She wants him to cut into her line,
in front of her. He wipes away the sweat.
He just can't trust her, it's too illegal,
he holds his place. Then Line B moves again.

He stares ahead, down the narrow corridor.
This is where they told him to stand and wait
to get his papers, his documents.
It seems he has a wife and kids somewhere,
a job, a mother who's very ill ....
Someone speaks, another complaint:
"I'm sick of this! I've got a life to live!"
Then Line B moves. The blonde moves around the corner.

Books

"Pictures *are* my friends—I have none others,"
wrote Ruskin, who also worshipped empty-headed
little girls. And Music also keeps good company,
but as Dr. Johnson pointed out, it gives
"no new ideas." But surely, People make
the poorest friends of all, refusing to be decent.
So Books became his only friends: he embraced
their words, and lent his volumes to no one.

But when he travels, he dreams of Alexandria,
or Fascist burnings, and grows in phobic fear,
having believed the tale of the book that was shot
and slowly bled to death. And once he hosted a party,
and most of the people who should have come, did not,
but *all* of his books were there, enjoying themselves
immensely, murmuring lightly, discussing so many things
from so many different and interesting points of view.

CREMATORIUM

She put $200 in his hand,
"I'd like to buy another bowl of ashes."
He quickly put the money away and gave her,
without question, exactly what she wanted.
The "burning" had been her husband's final insult—
he *knew* she didn't approve—in thirty years
of subtle cruelties, which she bore in silence,
thirty years of ashes in her mouth.

But he loved his boat and the ocean breeze,
and directed the family to spread his ashes
into the Sound near Bayville, which they did,
never to know that one dark night, months later,
while walking the dog on the sleeping Jackson's lawn,
she stopped above their broken septic tank,
and then, without the slightest vindictiveness,
she poured him in—right where he belonged.

A Rebours

"Nothing was visible on the surface"

—J. K. Huysmans

To travel ahead he had to leave behind
the sensate pleasures of the cottage life
at Fontenay—its decadent books and flowers,
and all the delicate plates of Jan Luyken—
to mix amid these boisterous foreign swarms
which rudely drank their port at the "Bodega"
in Paris, in the rain, "imagining"
his trip abroad among such chattering people.

But then, before departure, he recalled
that tour he took of Holland in his youth—
no scenes like Teniers' or like Jan Steen's,
but only crushing disillusionment.
He rose, at once, to leave. To go back home,
from where the greater journey would commence
beyond the muzzle of a loaded gun
for something else, final, against the grain.

Hospitals

She never went inside. Spooked by all
the blood, machines, and drugs, and all the clean
white halls and surgery rooms. So, every time,
she waited in the car outside, or stayed at home.
Even when her father slowly died,
but every day, they talked for hours on the phone,
until she could arrange to bring him home,
to die in peace. He seemed to understand.

Today, she says, "I have to go for tests,"
then calmly walks into the lobby,
convinced she has the cancer too, and whispers
to her husband—who's stunned and terrified,
who waits alone in a room with magazines,
until the doctor comes: "*Yes*, she's right ..."
but, still, she "might" survive, she just might "beat it ..."
but all he heard was the whisper, "It's my turn."

The Hudson Guild Theatre

Unexpectedly, at intermission,
he saw her face across the crowded lobby.
He'd come, tonight, with friends: the much-praised play
was dramaless, contemporary, and dull,
but she was wonderful, in every way,
even after all these years, and seemingly
content, standing with her second husband,
(he had been the first). Beautiful.

Back when they'd broken apart, their friends agreed
that it was "neither's fault," but they both knew
it was. They'd let it go. They'd hurt each other,
then simply let it go. And now, he couldn't
bear to see her face to face because
she might, like him, succumb into this ugly,
nauseous, guilty pain. And so, he left,
and never asked what happened in the second act.

ADRIATIC

She wakes, alone, on the cruise ship's highest deck,
lying in a chair, beneath the night.
Despite his promises, he isn't there.
The night is cool with patchy, floating fog;
the ship, deserted, seems to drift without
direction. Tonight, she'd rushed into Brindisi,
the harbor city of pestilence and quakes,
and bought her ticket and rushed on board.

Now drifting on the silent seas alone,
she wonders if she bought the proper passage.
Drifting south and east, she doesn't really care.
She might arrive in Corinth, maybe not.
She dreams of Crete and Rhodes, Izmir,
and Haifa ... even Alexandria.
It doesn't really matter; she feels content—
as if she's slowly drifting in the right direction.

5

CONFIDENCE MAN

Casually, he glanced across the courtroom,
checking out the nine dimwitted jurors.
The foxy chick in the designer clothes
reminded him of an early mark, years ago,
in Baltimore, his second Pigeon Drop.
Those were the days—with all the classic bunco:
Jamaican Hustles, the Indian Penny Scam,
the Violin, the Diamond Ring, and the Missing Heir.

While other kids went off to loaf at college,
he played the sucker scams, respecting only
those who didn't take the bait up-front,
and he had other standards too: no charity fraud,
no elderly marks, no disaster victims.
He also never used his charm and "knock-out" looks
for quickie sex with eager female dupes.
Business was business, and sex was a different scam.

He glanced at both his "victims" (plaintiffs),
Mr. Jerk and Mrs. Bitch, and managed
not to smile. He'd sold the greedy bastards
600 acres of prime Nevada wasteland,
for "oil leasing," at 500 bucks an acre—
which cost him 3 apiece—where the only oil,
for 200 miles, was lubing through the tourist
vans that cruised down Highway 41.

He'd met them at the Pineview Country Club
on a Friday night and closed the deal on Monday,
and *that* was the "kick," the personal payoff:
not the money, but watching their pathetic greed
expand to something inexhaustibly grotesque,

until the "blow off" finally came, and left
them devastated, humiliated, and crushed—
exactly as they both deserved to be.

And now, the Feds had brought him back in chains,
from Honolulu, after the fluke arrest—
Mrs. Bitch's vacationing sister had seen him
dining at the elegant Kulu in Waikiki—
and yet, despite what everyone might think,
he was enjoying himself. Sure he was clever,
and handsome, and quite an actor, but he was also
the foremost master of the "paperless" trail.

They'd never even know about the "super" stuff—
the shelter frauds, computer scams, and precious
metal rip-offs—or the millions in Zurich,
the condos, or the Mediterranean villas.
They'd also never know that he *loved* this "house of cards,"
the U.S. courts—the biggest scam of all—
where nothing counts but brass, deception, and fraud,
some things he knew a little bit about.

An "expert" shrink, another kind of con,
was talking in the witness box
about his manic and depressive states,
wild delusions, personality splits,
and his abusive, dysfunctional parents.
Again, he kept from smiling, even laughing;
he'd never been depressed in his whole life,
and mom and dad—rest in peace—were perfect saints.

"Mr. Wesley might appear contrite,"
the D.A. later said in his summation,
"but he's a ruthless wrecker of peoples' lives."
Remorsefully, "Wesley" looked around—
these morons didn't even know his name,
or the sixteen other false identities,

or the wife (with kids) in Jersey, or the one
in Vegas, or the latest one on Maui.

Sentence: two months suspended, three community service,
repay the money, cover their legal fees,
and suffer through the lecture by the judge. Not bad.
He *loved* this country—the land of marks and suckers,
with all its mushy laws, and covetousness,
its freedom to do most any damned thing
under the sun, and its judiciary con,
where one, with certain skills, could scam the scam.

▾ **6** ▾

Aliens

In, then out, of deep hypnotic regression,
she told her sympathetic Harvard research prof
about the ship's white, sterile room
in which they'd probed her naked body as
she lay out flat and perfectly immobile
in order to assist the world—
her Ivy League psychiatrist explained—
to reach a higher level of consciousness.

But never did she reveal—she recollected later,
driving past that selfish bastard Bob's
new condo, with a condescending sneer—
that one of her abductors had attempted
to impregnate her, and just how good it felt,
both then and now, to be more special
than anyone else on earth—who'd had the world's
(the galaxy's) most extraordinary lover.

MUNICH

"Du musst dein Leben ändern"

—Rilke

He never tells her, when she sometimes asks,
what he remembers most of that summer month
in Munich, years ago, when they first met.
Because he always remembers the Warsaw train,
the night before he arrived, and passing by
that strange young Prussian girl in the dining car,
sitting alone, dressed in white and pink,
like fresh carnations, with a black arm band.

Her grief, it seemed, had been thrust upon her;
she sat in silence, reading Rilke's poems.
And when he passed, their eyes met for a moment—
he fell into her grief—but she looked away.
Later that night, and finding no sleep nor rest,
he returned to the dining car, but she was gone—
but she'd left behind the poems, which he read
until dawn, over and over, unsatisfied.

TELEPHONE PSYCHIC

"He'll be very kind and thoughtful and he'll *love*
the movies!" Picking up her envelope,
she glanced across her long red nails, "You'll meet
him in the next few months." She truly *loved*
this job, always using her imagination.
She took her paycheck out and winked at Connie
in the corner cubicle. As long as "Jane" believes
that something will happen, then, probably, it will.

Oh sure, it's all a "lie"—as mom so bluntly
puts it—yet it's just a kind of "whitish" lie:
putting her clients in a healthy frame of mind.
Like when her dad would call to tell her that
his tests were negative; or when her son
would reassure her that he'd given up the drugs;
or when, tonight, her husband called from Al's
Blue Star Motel to say he's working late.

TRAUMA CENTER

They flew him in by chopper late last night:
the slug, a .38, had missed his heart,
but left a bloody, mangled mess inside.
More than once, he'd saved this punk before,
the eldest of the infamous Davis brothers,
a violent pimp and pusher who'd told him once,
"I'm indestructible, man," and then, one other
time, "I've put six suckers in the box."

At 6:00 A.M., the apprehensive surgeon
rechecked the room, which was, as he expected,
empty. Once again, the man had yanked
away his IV lines and risen up,
with the hole right through his chest, and slithered back
into the Newark streets, looking for "action,"
drugs, and prey—amid your sons and daughters—
exactly where the surgeon's knife had put him.

MONTE CARLO

The chic American girl, unescorted,
waits in the elegant *salon privé.*
The house has cleared the bet. Two million francs.
She puts it on *"noir"* and watches the wheel,
as everyone watches her. "The betting is closed."
Despite Pascal, despite the theory of large numbers,
she's known to be a careful "system" player—
decisive, sure, and confident. Yet, not really:

If "red," she loses everything she has;
she'll have to meet the count in Saint-Tropez.
If "black," she wins; she'll take her handsome Greek
to Paros for the month of June.
With little interest, she watches the wheel. *"Zero!"*
One in thirty-seven. The house wins. She leaves—
to do what she has always done on zero:
go back home and see her mom in Maine.

EAST RIVER

He sat at the Brooklyn end of the bridge
and stared below into the dark East River.
Forty years ago, his father tried to jump,
not even sure if it would take his life.
His fiancée had left him only a note—
full of strange, incomprehensible darkness—
then sailed back home, alone, to Bucovice
where life was hard but, nevertheless, was home.

And now, tonight, his father was dead;
the cancer like a black and flowing river.
He lifted his eyes up to the blazing city:
"It gives you what you're worth," his father would say,
of the city he loved, when life, even here, was hard.
And then, from across the river, he heard the siren—
an ambulance racing through the city nights
taking away the ones we love.

COUNTRY CLUB

Another little triumph. And now, she comes,
tan, and glistening with sweat, from the tennis courts.
Remarkable. And perfect in her ways.
He watches her, his wife, like everyone else.
And thinks of all they have: the brand new home
"out" in the Hamptons—friends, and status, and comfort.
But soon, he knows, they'll be packing up their things.
He sees it in her eyes. She's restless again.

And once he asked her why. Was that in Saint-
Tropez, or Hilton Head, or Malibu?
He thought it might have come from the weary childhood,
unsettled, moving from place to place to place.
"I like it here—*much too much*—to die here."
"But we're not sick, or old. We might live on
for decades." But then, she wipes the sweat from her face,
restless once again. "But we might not."

DISPHOBIC

It's comforting to live one's life without
identifiable, phobic problems.—
Like Jeanne, who hasn't flown a plane in years
because the very thought will palpitate
her heart until she hyperventilates,
with cold adrenaline gushing into her veins,
with nausea and debilitating freezing sweats,
until she wishes she were dead.

Like Anthony, who panics in the dark,
or Jack, who dreads the smell and look of fire,
or Mary Ann, who never leaves her house.—
But what's it called when someone has the dark
and terrifying fear that all his sins
relentlessly, are stalking in the night,
all the more brazen for not having
a recognizable, scientific name?

SUICIDE NOTE

The night that she committed suicide:
her brother in New Jersey played the horses,
drinking with his buddies all night long;
her friend at Yale thumbed through a recent novel
looking in vain for meaning and for love;
her mother was asleep in New Rochelle;
her father, dead, was knocking on his box,
hoping to distract his little girl.

Her former lover, somewhere at the Cape,
was lying with a pretty undergrad,
content to think of anything but her.
Then someone read the poem beside the body,
which completely ignored the darkness in her mind,
or why her suicidal note was blank,
as everyone hurtled through the dark of space
sitting on their little, moist, blue rock.

▾ *7* ▾

Obituary in *The New York Times*

Today he read the notice of a death
buried deep within *The New York Times*.
Concise and brief, just 87 words,
it read, he knew, exactly like his own.
Some unknown man, his age, who'd died of cancer—
and he wondered if *his* children ever called,
and if *his* late divorce had left the woman
as bitter and unforgiving as his first wife.

He wondered if *his* "freedom" was empty and cold,
and if he had more wealth than he could need—
and if he had sometime, just recently,
discovered that almost everything
he'd ever said and thought, throughout his life,
was totally wrong and self-indulgent.
Then, as he felt his cancer surge within,
he wondered if the same kind took *him* down.

ISCHIA

The third night on the island, we saw her walking
the colonnades, beautiful in blue,
beyond the harbor lights, and searching for *you*.
And other nights, we saw her wander past
the altars of Apollo, or near the springs,
or even through the dangerous earthquake ruins.
They said she was the "inconsolable" one,
and everyone, it seemed, wished to have her love.

And then one night, we found her on the beaches,
watching the eerie, blue Tyrrhenian Sea,
and as we wondered what to say, she said:
"I search for someone yet to come."—
At dawn, from the deck, as the ship set sail,
we watched her island fade beyond the sea
and thought of *you*, whoever you might be,
and if, ever, you could deserve her deep, blue love.

rec.antiques

Every single night, and weekends too,
he talked by type on Internet about
antiques. Of course, he'd read the articles
about those "hooked" on cyberspace—dependent,
isolated, and needing a "life." But he
was perfectly content within his condo,
in Silicon Valley, until she flew to the coast
to meet him at the Oakridge Antiques Forum.

Surreptitiously, and damp with sweat,
he watched her sitting alone, and beautiful,
where they had planned to meet. Again, he wondered
if he'd made the right decision. The page
walked up and handed her the note she quickly
read before she rose and walked away:
"Sorry I couldn't come. A death in the family.
P.S.: Will contact you tonight on Internet."

Runway

Was it really her he saw last night?
Sitting in a limousine on 67th
Street near Tavern on the Green?
Expressionless, yet just as beautiful
as twenty years ago, when he'd pursued her
at the Jersey shore. Until one night
she said, "All right," and took him to the airport
at two A.M. and climbed beneath the fence.

Then, side by side, they lay down in a ditch
in front of Runway 12. She held him close,
and then he saw it, huge, with flashing lights,
descending from the sky, like a bird of prey,
tremendous, closer, falling down upon them,
then roaring over their heads onto the runway—
and she looked into his eyes, as if to say,
"*This* is what life with me is like!"

SOUTH SHORE COTTAGE

At dawn, he came back down to the water's edge,
and even in the early morning winds,
its burning stench still lingered in the air:
black, ashes—everything was blackened rubble,
the roof was gone, and all the walls were down.
It was what he'd become—what he deserved—
and as the waves came in, the gulls cried out,
and, once again, he wondered where you were.

Then, standing there amid the smoking ruins,
he saw the charred remains of a figurine,
something of yours, a dancing girl,
broken and fired black in the orange embers.
He wondered if the glass would burn his hands,
but when he touched it gently, it did not—
but still he needed you now, more than ever,
to bandage up his scalded, empty hands.

BABYSNATCHER

At any time, she could, of course, walk over
to her car and drive away. Later,
she heard the sirens and the motorcycles,
kissed the child, and handed it to a cop.
Someone read her rights, but no one cuffed her hands.
Finally, the mother arrived and held her baby.
In shock, the mother glared across the park
into her eyes, staring as one would stare at a monster.

But she'll get "two months" at most. She'll tell the judge
about her wasted years, her countless rotten lovers,
her barrenness, and her mental instability.
She'll serve her time, then move to a distant state,
and do it again: since holding a stolen child,
and feeling its beating heart, will usually last
about two years, especially since she could, of course,
walk over to her car and drive away.

MAIN READING ROOM

Worn out, he pushed the Renaissance aside:
Die Kulture, Burckhardt's great Italian dreams—
what better way to pass this rainy day?
But tired now, he needed a little walk,
and rest, and since the reading room was mostly
full of books and academics, he wandered
down the empty corridors, until
he saw them standing there, alone, together:

Young lovers, waiting out the August rain—
drenched, lost in her hair, he held her close,
who pressed her open mouth across his neck....
Later, in the quiet reading room,
for all the rest of that long day and night,
he thought of you, and fifteen years ago—
the smell of your hair in the north shore summer night,
your tender touch, your warm, wet, wild mouth.

SUMMER IN THE CYCLADES

Uneasy, here, within these Grecian islands:
Naxos, Delos, even perfect Paros,
with all their sun, and their blue Aegean Sea—
yet she was strangely disaffected here,
a kind of loss of equilibrium,
and then, one summer night like all the rest,
the sudden message came: "An accident."
Her closest friend, Marie, was dead.

She flew into Manhattan the following day,
but called no one when she arrived. Instead,
she shopped past noon at Saks, then browsed the Frick
until her daiquiris at Essex House,
then rested in the park behind the Met.
In balance, once again, she now could try
to face the thing—and walk into the wake
to grieve, incomprehensible, her loss.

THE SHIPMASTER'S NOTE

The Arctic

To whom it may concern: we're trapped within
these everlasting ices of the north.
Tonight, I bother to dictate this note,
not because we might all starve and perish,
but because of what I've seen: madness.
The first one came two days ago, with sledge and dogs.
He keeps his distance but, at night,
I've heard him cry, "Come Victor, follow me."

The second one arrived today, half dead.
A doctor who'd tampered with the source of life,
conceived a creature in his own self-interest,
and then rejected the very one he'd made,
without compassion, without love. Despite
his health, he plans to chase his "daemon." Fine.
Let him go. This is the frozen place of death
for one such monster to pursue the other.

About the Author

William Baer, a graduate of Rutgers and New York University, wrote his dissertation at the University of South Carolina under the direction of James Dickey. He later attended the Writing Seminars at The Johns Hopkins University and has been the recipient of a Fulbright and a National Endowment for the Arts Creative Writing Grant. His work has been published in *Poetry, The Hudson Review, Ploughshares, The Southern Review, The New Criterion,* and many other literary journals.

Design and typography by Timothy Rolands
Cover design by Teresa Wheeler

The poems are set in ITC Legacy Serif,
a revival of Nicolas Jenson's roman
designed by Ronald Arnholm.
Titles are set in Mantinia,
designed by Matthew Carter.

This book was printed and bound
by Thomson-Shore, Dexter, Michigan.